JOURNEY of the WHARFE

HILLSIDE GUIDES
....cover much of Northern England

Journeys
- JOURNEY OF THE AIRE • JOURNEY OF THE WHARFE
- JOURNEY OF THE URE *(in preparation)*

Short Scenic Walks *(average 4 miles)*
- UPPER WHARFEDALE • LOWER WHARFEDALE
- UPPER WENSLEYDALE • LOWER WENSLEYDALE
- MALHAMDALE • SWALEDALE • RIBBLESDALE
- INGLETON/WESTERN DALES • SEDBERGH/DENTDALE
- NIDDERDALE • HARROGATE/KNARESBOROUGH
- BOWLAND • AROUND PENDLE • RIBBLE VALLEY
- BORROWDALE • HAWORTH/BRONTE COUNTRY
- ILKLEY/WASHBURN VALLEY • AMBLESIDE/LANGDALE
- AIRE VALLEY • HEBDEN BRIDGE/CALDER VALLEY

Walking Country *(average 6 miles)*
- WHARFEDALE & MALHAM • NIDDERDALE & RIPON
- THREE PEAKS & HOWGILL FELLS • ILKLEY MOOR
- WENSLEYDALE • HARROGATE & the WHARFE VALLEY
- SWALEDALE • EDEN VALLEY • ALSTON & ALLENDALE
- BRONTE COUNTRY • CALDERDALE • BOWLAND
- HOWARDIAN HILLS • ARNSIDE & SILVERDALE
- PENDLE & the RIBBLE • LUNESDALE
- NORTH YORK MOORS, SOUTH & WEST
- NORTH YORK MOORS, NORTH & EAST

Long Distance Walks
- COAST TO COAST WALK • CUMBRIA WAY • DALES WAY
- BRONTE WAY • PENDLE WAY • CALDERDALE WAY

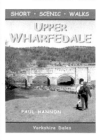
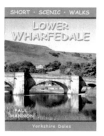
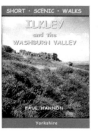

JOURNEY OF
THE WHARFE

Portrait of a Yorkshire River
Paul Hannon

HILLSIDE PUBLICATIONS
20 Wheathead Crescent
Keighley
West Yorkshire
BD22 6LX

First Published 2014

© Paul Hannon 2014

ISBN 978 1 907626 13 5

Visit www.hillsidepublications.co.uk

Illustrations:
Front Cover: Bolton Abbey
Back Cover: Cow & Calf Rocks, Ilkley Moor
Page 1: Burnsall Bridge and Burnsall Fell
Page 2: Kilnsey Crag
Page 3: River Wharfe at Conistone
Page 4: Winter at Barden
Opposite:
Row 1: Buckden Pike; Cote Gill, Hawkswick
Row 2: Upper Wharfedale; Bolton Abbey station
Row 3: Denton; Otley
Row 4: Arthington Show; Bramham Horse Trials
(Paul Hannon/Yorkshire Photo Library)

Printed in China on behalf of Latitude Press

CONTENTS

INTRODUCTION

Best loved of all Yorkshire rivers, the Wharfe flows 60 glorious miles from Cam Fell in the heart of the Dales to join the River Ouse at Wharfe's Mouth, near Cawood in the Vale of York. Little of Wharfeland needs an introduction, the upper half being a litany of illustrious Dales names such as Kettlewell, Arncliffe and Linton, while the lower half is spread between a quartet of much-loved small towns.

In the very centre of the Yorkshire Dales National Park, two lonely becks emerge from bleak uplands to form our river. Opening miles through the medieval hunting forest of Langstrothdale Chase see it turn for a long and spritely journey through Upper Wharfedale, running between high, sprawling fells before absorbing the equally delectable Skirfare from Littondale in the shadow of Kilnsey Crag. Gleaming limestone flanks usher the Wharfe through to the charms of Grass Wood, above which Grassington Moor bears reminders of a once thriving lead mining industry. Perhaps the finest stage of all sees mile after mile of beautiful riverside paths lead through Burnsall and Appletreewick to Barden Tower and Bolton Abbey, where rich woodland sits beneath spacious heather moorland.

Below Bolton Bridge the Wharfe meets the first of its towns, as the perennial Yorkshire icon of Ilkley shelters beneath its world famous moor. Only a little further and enterprising Otley punches well above its weight, it too sheltering beneath its own skyline of the Chevin. Second tributary river the Washburn arrives from its reservoir-jewelled valley, and now slopes relent to reveal features as varied as the landmark Almscliff Crag and the grandiose Harewood House. Wetherby's racecourse sits alongside the Great North Road, and the northern brewing capital of Tadcaster sends the Wharfe on its final, lazy miles.

These pages capture the life and landscape of the River Wharfe's richly varied catchment area, from wild uplands to pretty villages, and showcase a diverse range of events and attractions that help keep our countryside alive.

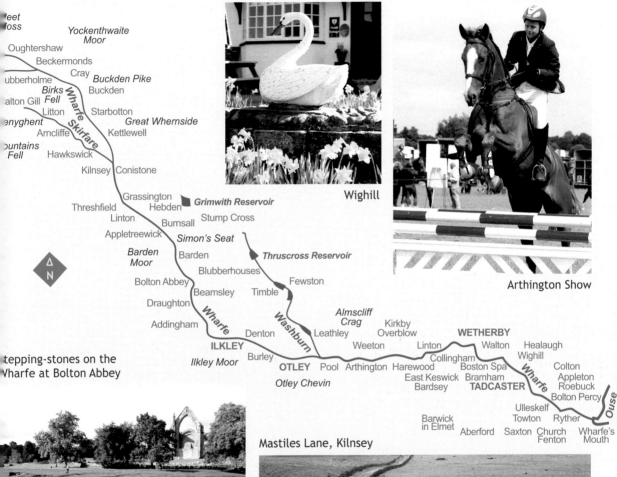

eet oss
Yockenthwaite Moor
Oughtershaw
Beckermonds
Cray
Buckden Pike
ubberholme
Birks Fell
Buckden
alton Gill
Litton
Starbotton
enyghent
Wharfe
Skirfare
Great Whernside
Arncliffe
Kettlewell
untains Fell
Hawkswick
Kilnsey
Conistone
Grassington
Threshfield
Hebden
Grimwith Reservoir
Linton
Stump Cross
Burnsall
Appletreewick
Simon's Seat
Barden Moor
Barden
Thruscross Reservoir
Blubberhouses
Bolton Abbey
Beamsley
Timble
Fewston
Draughton
Addingham
Wharfe
Washburn
Almscliff Crag
Denton
Leathley
Kirkby Overblow
WETHERBY
ILKLEY
Weeton
Linton
Walton
Healaugh
Burley
Wighill
Ilkley Moor
OTLEY
Pool
Arthington
Harewood
Collingham
Boston Spa
Colton
Appleton Roebuck
Otley Chevin
East Keswick
Bardsey
Bramham
TADCASTER
Bolton Percy
Ouse
Ulleskelf
Towton
Ryther
Wharfe's Mouth
Barwick in Elmet
Aberford
Saxton
Church Fenton
Wharfe

Wighill

Arthington Show

Mastiles Lane, Kilnsey

tepping-stones on the Wharfe at Bolton Abbey

1 LANGSTROTHDALE

THE LONELY LANDSCAPE........

The opening miles of the Wharfe, from its beginnings on Cam Fell down to Buckden are known as Langstrothdale, an upland valley of lonely farming hamlets nestled beneath even lonelier high fells. Geographically this is at the very heart of the Yorkshire Dales: the

River Ribble is born within a stone's throw of the Wharfe, but the vagaries of a peaty Pennine watershed send its waters flowing westwards instead. Formed at Beckermonds by the meeting of Oughtershaw Beck and Greenfield Beck, the Wharfe exhibits an immediately youthful exuberance as it travels the slender valley floor. The narrow road that shadows it escapes to climb a tortuous route over the tops and down to Hawes, at the head of Wensleydale.

First pub in Wharfedale at Hubberholme;
Hazy moon over Buckden;
Morning mist leaving Buckden
Opposite: The Wharfe below Beckermonds; Autumn rainbow near Yockenthwaite

BECKERMONDS

At Beckermonds the meeting of Oughtershaw and Greenfield Becks marks the creation of the Wharfe, a charming spot where wagtails play by grassy banks. Each beck has already covered some mileage to provide a fair volume of water for the Wharfe's birth. The former passes through the valley's first hamlet at Oughtershaw huddled beneath Fleet Moss, while the latter starts near the extremely isolated farm of High Green Field, almost submerged in silent forests.

Oughtershaw and Oughtershaw Beck

High Green Field; The confluence at Beckermonds;
Sunset over Ingleborough from the climb to Fleet Moss

DEEPDALE

The newly-formed Wharfe revels in the infancy of its first miles through lovely Langstrothdale, tumbling joyously over low limestone ledges yet in drier times, completely sinking below ground. Downstream of the farming hamlet of Deepdale is a modest stone circle: just 20ft in diameter, this compact grouping of 30 stones enjoys a noble riverside setting seen by few motorists from the opposite bank.

Langstrothdale seasons and the stone circle

YOCKENTHWAITE

This farming hamlet occupies a magnificent setting within the medieval hunting forest of Langstrothdale Chase. Much earlier still, 'Eogan's clearing' was named by the Norsemen who settled here. Immediately upstream the Wharfe often sinks below ground, while slopes behind rise to more than 2000ft on the peaty plateau of Yockenthwaite Moor, bedecked with an array of jewelled tarns amid otherwise inhospitable terrain.

Waterfall under Yockenthwaite Moor;
Cotton-grass at Oughtershaw Tarn
Opposite: Bridge and dry river-bed;
Yockenthwaite

HUBBERHOLME

Barely a hamlet, Hubberholme boasts two famous buildings and a shapely bridge which connects them. This highest church in the dale has a tower showing Norman traces, while a 500-year old oak rood loft is one of only two remaining in Yorkshire. Bradford writer J B Priestley chose wisely in having his ashes scattered hereabouts. Across the river is the whitewashed and homely George Inn, which formerly housed the vicar. Its flagged floors continue to be the scene of the New Year land-letting, the auction of a 'poor pasture' which originally raised funds for needy parishioners.

St Michael's church, and sheep waiting to be relieved of their fleeces at the adjacent farm

CRAY

Occupying a delightful terrace at over 1000 feet above sea level, the tiny farming hamlet of Cray is the very last outpost of Wharfedale on the pass leading over Kidstones to Bishopdale, the easiest motorable route out of the valley northwards of Grassington. The White Lion is a welcoming pub with a stone-flagged floor.

A wartime giant lumbers above Cray, also viewed from the more down-to-earth snowy platform of Buckden Rake

BUCKDEN

At the meeting place of two high roads from Wensleydale, Buckden is the first village to be encountered by the Wharfe. In medieval times it was the administrative centre of a vast hunting forest, and the Buck Inn recalls that importance. The village stands on the slopes of Buckden Pike, and swift-flowing Buckden Beck carves a deep defile down from the summit. For more genteel pedestrians, a stony track makes its way up Buckden Rake towards Cray on a section of Roman road that connected forts at Ilkley and Bainbridge.

Springtime in Buckden, and autumn on Buckden Bridge

Buckden Pike

Outwith the Three Peaks this is the most popular of Dales fells, due in part to a wealth of interesting ascent paths. At 2303ft/702m it boasts extensive views both into and far out of the Dales. Buckden Gill links village and summit, and features splendid waterfalls and haunting lead mining remains. High on the summit ridge is a landmark cross erected by a Polish airman, the lone survivor of a wartime plane crash.

Memorial cross and Buckden Gill

High on Buckden Pike, with the main picture looking up-dale to Hubberholme

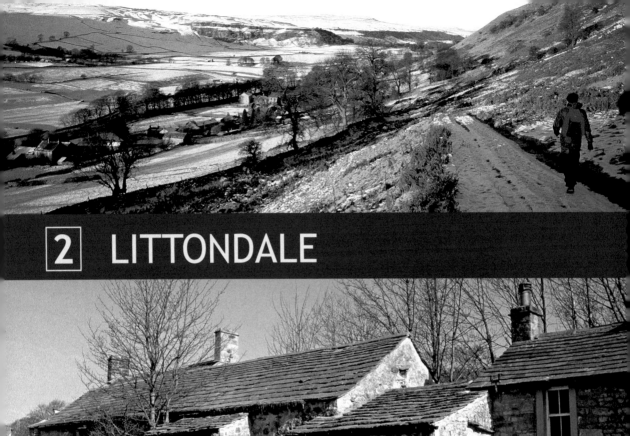

2 LITTONDALE

A CHIP OFF THE OLD BLOCK........

Lovely Littondale runs just a few short miles from the old farmstead of Cosh to its meeting with the Wharfe near Kilnsey. Here at Amerdale Dub the River Skirfare completes its journey having shunned virtually all publicity. Even its tiny villages see little of it, only at the Littondale 'capital' of Arncliffe does the river flow by its church. The dale is named from its other notable village of Litton, rather than its river, and in times past was also known as Amerdale. Several 2000ft fells crowd in, most noteworthy being mighty Penyghent, normally only associated with Ribblesdale. Littondale's flat valley floor and steep flanks replicate the main valley to the east, indeed from the vantage point of Conistone Pie above Conistone, they resemble identical twins. Even in this short valley, two moorland motor roads escape out to Malham Tarn and to Stainforth on the Ribble.

The dalehead farm of Foxup; Limestone scars at Cowside
Opposite: Winter descent to Hawkswick from Hawkswick Moor;
Springtime on the village green at Arncliffe

23

Halton Gill

The first settlement of any size in Littondale is this cluster of grey buildings nestled at the foot of Horse Head Pass on the mighty Birks Fell ridge. The green road of the pass was once a regular route of Halton Gill's curate, who crossed on horseback to take services at Hubberholme. Facing Halton Gill is 2231ft/680m Plover Hill, looking out over the ravagingly bleak upper reaches of Littondale which include the old farms of Foxup and Cosh.

Sheep on the street and high above Foxup;
Summit snowdrift on Plover Hill
　　　　Opposite: Halton Gill amid summer meadows;
and seen beneath Horse Head from Hesleden Bergh

PENYGHENT

At 2277ft/694m the crouching lion of Penyghent is a majestic mountain, though comparatively few will know the eastern flanks that fall to Littondale. While most ascents spring from Horton-in-Ribblesdale, all will tread the Littondale side at some point, as the atmospheric summit is itself on our patch. This is also the only one of the Three Peaks traversed by the Pennine Way.

Fountains Fell from Penyghent;
Ascending the south ridge
Opposite: Penyghent from Crooke Gill

LITTON

Litton is only the second largest village in the dale of the River Skirfare, but can boast that it gave its name to this valley once known as Amerdale. Its attractive buildings ranged along the road include the whitewashed and welcoming Queens Arms. The river is regularly dry hereabouts, having gone subterranean some distance upstream.

Across the valley rises Darnbrook Fell, lesser known sidekick of Fountains Fell which lurks behind. Named from its former owners the Cistercian monks of Fountains Abbey, their great sheep runs covered great swathes of the Dales, while coal mining took place virtually on the summit plateau. Traversing the flanks of these fells is the Dawson Close track, a classic green lane rising out of Litton towards Ribblesdale.

The contrasting summits of Darnbrook Fell (right) and Fountains Fell (below), both looking to Penyghent
Opposite: The Skirfare at Litton; Mountain biker on the Dawson Close track; Winter at Litton

28

ARNCLIFFE

The 'capital' of Littondale is one of the most attractive villages in the Dales. Characterful houses stand back in relaxed manner from a spacious green. The unpretentious Falcon maintains this mood, the only pub in the area to serve its ale directly from the barrel. St Oswald's church stands embowered in trees in a beautiful riverside setting, while the house at Bridge End played host to Charles Kingsley while writing 'The Water Babies'.

River Skirfare; Falcon Inn
Opposite: Old Cotes; Bridge

HAWKSWICK

Strung along a back road, the few cottages and farm buildings of Littondale's last village remain wonderfully undisturbed. The slopes of Hawkswick Clowder across the river feature caves, ancient settlements and limestone pavements.

Hut circle on Dowkabottom; Caver emerging from Dowkabottom Cave; Hawkswick from across the Skirfare

Looking over Hawkswick Moor to Great Whernside from Cote Gill

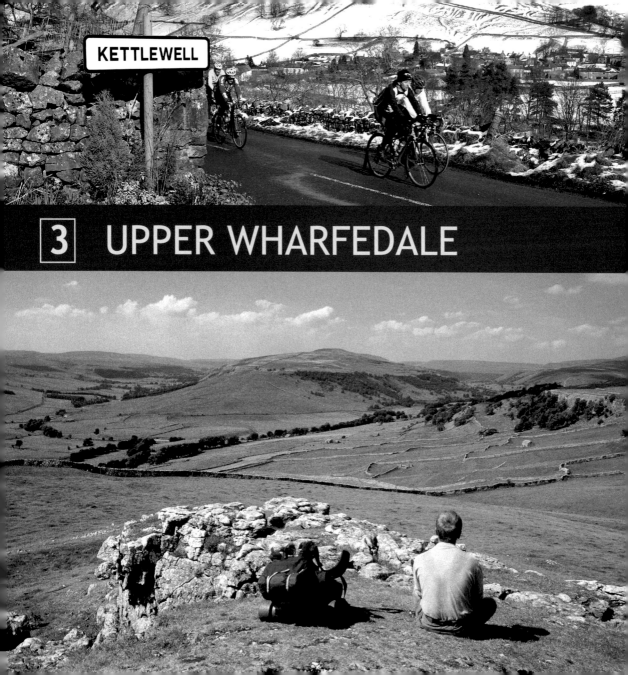

3 UPPER WHARFEDALE

LIMESTONE COUNTRY OF THE WHARFE........

From Kettlewell to Linton, Upper Wharfedale offers a roll-call of magical names. At its heart, Grassington embraces everything, from the foaming river at Ghaistrill's Strid, up through mercurial Grass Wood to its sweeping moor, scene of intense 19th century lead mining activity. Less feted villages like Conistone, Threshfield and Hebden hide a wealth of fascinating features in their immediate hinterlands, and the monastic highway of Mastiles Lane still climbs high above Kilnsey towards Malham. Proud patriarch of the upper dale is the mountain-mass of Great Whernside, while Kilnsey's remarkable crag is a major showpiece of the dale. The dominant limestone is evident in the many miles of scars, pavements and ravines which seam the valley sides and uplands.

Pictorial inn signs at Linton and Starbotton; Fishing lake at Kilnsey
Opposite: Kettlewell;
Littondale and Wharfedale
from Conistone Pie

STARBOTTON

A whitewashed pub and a Quaker burial ground are features of this village with lovely cottages bearing 17th century datestones. Starbotton nestles beneath Buckden Pike on swift-flowing Cam Gill Beck, which cuts a deep groove in the flank of the fell. These lower slopes have a ruined smelt mill chimney from lead mining days.

Village corners of Starbotton; Starbotton, Buckden Pike and the Wharfe from Moor End

Great Whernside

Wharfedale's highest fell is also its bulkiest, innumerable square miles of moorland falling eastwards into the empty upper reaches of Nidderdale. Only from Kettlewell is there easy access, popular routes leading via Providence Pot and Hag Dyke to the summit, where the line of Long Crags is crowned by an immense cairn. In the folds of Dowber Gill, Providence Pot is key to a labyrinthine cave system: an incongruous manhole cover guards the vertical shaft. At 1510ft/460m on the shelf above, Hag Dyke is one of the country's highest buildings, long used as a scouts' outdoor centre. From Kettlewell the tortuous Park Rash road climbs high over the fell's north-western flank bound for Middleham.

Winter on Park Rash; Ascending Hag Dyke Edge

KETTLEWELL

The principal village of the upper dale sits astride what was a major coaching route to Richmond, and its central inns would have serviced weary travellers, as they still do today. Kettlewell was a 19th century lead mining centre, and the beck racing through is lined by cottages which once housed miners. St Mary's church takes a back seat, with the village stocks and maypole nearby. The village is immensely popular with walkers: footpaths radiate in every direction, by riverbank, fields, up narrow gills, over the moors, limestone shelves and onto the heights, of which Great Whernside takes a paternal interest. Kettlewell found 21st century fame as location for the hit movie 'Calendar Girls'.

Blue Bell; Descent from The Slit   Opposite: Dowber Gill; River Wharfe; Kettlewell from above Knipe Wood

KILNSEY

Kilnsey offers attractions far outweighing its hamlet status. It is renowned first and foremost for the stupendous rock architecture of Kilnsey Crag, a serious climbing arena of impossibly smooth limestone. This famous overhang broods over Kilnsey's other great draw, its annual show. In late summer the riverside pasture is alive with the colour of the dale's premier event. All manner of

attractions are overshadowed by the fell race, the objective of which is all too obvious! Up the hill behind the pub and Kilnsey Park's trout fishing is the Old Hall, built in Tudor times on the site of a grange of Fountains Abbey. Climbing directly out of the hamlet is Mastiles Lane, the big name in green roads of the Dales. Riding the rolling limestone uplands, it gave access to the valuable sheep grazing grounds of Malham for the Fountains' monks, continuing ultimately to their lands in Borrowdale, Cumberland.

Old Hall, Tennant Arms   Opposite: Kilnsey Crag and local hero Mick Hawkins ascending to victory in 1982

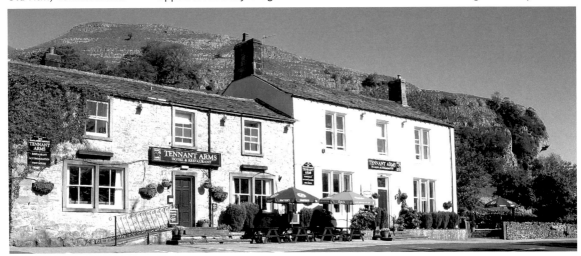

CONISTONE

This attractive little village features a tall maypole at its centre, while every block of stone in its old cottages matches the natural landscape of the village's hinterland. St Mary's church has a poignant memorial to the six victims of the Mossdale Cavern potholing disaster of 1967. Driving a deep wedge into the hillside is Conistone Dib, a classic dry valley narrowing to distinctive rock-girt termini. Higher again is more open limestone scenery, featuring scars, pavements, dewponds and wild flowers. Dib Scar is another limestone gorge.

Old Post office; The Wharfe at Conistone Bridge   Opposite: Above Conistone Dib; Kilnsey from Dib Scar; Church

GRASSINGTON

The capital of Upper Wharfedale is a busy community with a range of shops, pubs and cafes based around a cobbled square. Grassington boasted an 18th century theatre and a lead mining industry of which its moor still holds much evidence; here also is a folk museum. Annual events are the cultural extravaganza of the Grassington Festival in late June, and colourful Dickensian Saturdays in Advent. Grassington stands high above the river, whose delectable banks lead upstream to Ghaistrill's Strid. Here the briefly turbulent Wharfe is channelled through a ravine of waterworn rocks, though in spate the water rushes through and over the rocky shelves alongside.

Ghaistrill's Strid; River Wharfe

Dickensian Christmas; Foresters Arms;
Village cricket beneath a backdrop of Cracoe Fell

GRASSINGTON MOOR

Grassington Moor was one of the major centres of lead mining in the Dales, and along with the adjoining Pateley Bridge area it rivalled activities in Swaledale. Though dating back to Roman times, the industry peaked in the first half of the 19th century. Countless features of interest are scattered across the moor, most easily reached from the road-end at Yarnbury. Cupola Smelt Mill of 1793 was fired by locally won coal, and a long system of flues took poisonous fumes from the mill to a tall chimney. Between moor and river is Grass Wood, the largest individual remnant of native broadleaved woodland in the Dales, and blessed with a network of paths it is a particular delight in springtime.

Limestone pavement; Smelt mill chimney
Opposite: Workings on Grassington Moor;
River Wharfe from Grass Wood

HEBDEN

This hilly village climbs from an exhilarating suspension footbridge on the Wharfe up to rugged Hebden Gill on the very edge of Grassington Moor. In between these very contrasting features, the village centre has St Peter's church and a welcoming tearoom and pub. Like its bigger neighbour Grassington, Hebden grew with the lead mining industry, and Hebden Gill abounds in reminders of those hard days. The dense heather of Mossy Moor hides a modest stone circle, consisting of four major stones and eight in total.

Miners' bridge in Hebden Gill; Town Hill
Opposite: Stone circle; River Wharfe; Church

THRESHFIELD

This disjointed village is scattered around the junction of the Skipton-Grassington road with the valley road. Solid stone cottages and farm buildings overlook a triangular green, enclosed by walls and shrouded in trees. Inside are the old stocks, while across the road the Old Hall Inn's title reveals its origins. The village school stands down by the river, a lovely building that was originally a 17th century grammar school. Slopes behind the village rise through colourful Cow Close Wood to moorland where coal mining took place.

School and Cow Close Wood

Welcome to Threshfield!; Green; Milestones

LINTON-IN-CRAVEN

One of the north's most attractive villages sees an assortment of limestone buildings stood back from a spacious green. The pub name recalls local man Richard Fountaine, who made his fortune in London but remembered Linton by funding 18th century almshouses by the green. Through the green runs Linton Beck, crossed in quick succession by a road bridge, packhorse bridge, clapper bridge and ford. Down at Linton Falls the Wharfe crashes loudly over limestone ledges, a foaming sight in spate. In contrast, upstream it flows wide and calm between two weirs. Idyllically sited in a loop of the river is the church of St Michael & All Angels, with Norman origins.

Linton Falls and Church
Opposite: Four seasons on the village green

4 LOWER WHARFEDALE

WHARFE COUNTRY AT ITS VERY FINEST........

Perhaps the symbolic heart of Wharfeland is this truly exquisite few miles centred on the monastic grandeur of Bolton Abbey. From Burnsall to Bolton Bridge, a peerless riverbank leads amid rich woodland flanked by the gritstone portals of Barden Moor and Simon's Seat, whose slopes climb to undulating swathes of scented heather. Spectacular natural features include Troller's Gill, Stump Cross Caverns and the notorious Strid. Add to this Appletreewick with its street climbing by splendid pubs and old halls......, Strid Wood's abundant birds and trees......, the Cliffords' up-market hunting lodge of Barden Tower......, steam trains chugging across the low watershed from Embsay to Bolton Abbey......, Beamsley with its almshouses looking out to the mini-mountain of the Beacon...... Can Paradise match this?

The Red Lion at Burnsall beneath a range of old guideposts   Opposite: Barden Moor; Barden Bridge

GRIMWITH

Grimwith Reservoir was created in 1884 to supply Bradford, and a 1983 enlargement made it Yorkshire's largest expanse of inland water. Two attractive side gills, Gate Up Gill and Blea Gill formerly met above water level, and the drought of 1995 revealed the old bridge beneath where these met, oddly isolated amidst the sun-baked mud. A surround of rolling moorland makes a fine backdrop, particularly when draped in the purple heather of late summer.

Grimwith Reservoir in winter and in drought; Gate Up Gill

STUMP CROSS

Stump Cross Caverns are one of only three showcaves within the Dales, the other two being deep within the flanks of mighty Ingleborough. Discovered in 1860 by miners seeking lead, their efforts ultimately revealed an amazing labyrinth of tunnels and chambers with a fine display of stalactites and stalagmites that cannot fail to impress. The bleak exterior and remote moorland setting give no clues as to the wonders awaiting underground.

Stump Cross Caverns; Dusk over Wharfedale from Stump Cross

BURNSALL

Burnsall's setting is near perfection, with bridge, green, maypole, church, inn and cottages fusing together into an unforgettable Dales scene. St Wilfred's church dates largely from the 15th century, and alongside is the village school, founded in 1602 by William Craven as one of the earliest grammar schools. On the edge of the village the Wharfe rushes through a limestone fault at the gorge of Loup Scar.

Straight-talking sign;
Summer on the green;
Autumn by the Wharfe

Opposite: Loup Scar;
Church and school

BURNSALL FELL

Part of the all-embracing Barden Moor, Burnsall Fell hovers either protectively or menacingly, depending on the moods of the weather, over its village. In August the jolly, long-standing family event of Burnsall Sports features a classic fell-race, where athletes stretch sinews to ascend to the moor-top, thence to immediately return at alarmingly breakneck speed.

Burnsall from the fell   Opposite: Red grouse, local sheep - and the fell race

APPLETREEWICK

A delightful name for a lovely village with three old halls, two pubs and a tiny church. The Craven Arms takes its name from William Craven, a Dick Whittington character who made his fortune in London, becoming Lord Mayor in 1611: not forgetting his beginnings he had Burnsall's grammar school built. The pub's 21st century cruck barn is the first in the Dales for probably 300 years! The New Inn achieved national fame thanks to the 'no-smoking' policy of a 1970s landlord. On top of all this, the Wharfe itself is in splendid form hereabouts. At the farming hamlet of Skyreholme is 300-year old Parcevall Hall, with gardens open to the public. Behind it is the limestone gorge of Trollers Gill, whose normally dry, narrow passage is renowned as home of the Barguest, a spectral hound with eyes like saucers!

Rock climbing in Trollers Gill; Mock Beggar Hall; New Inn

Gardens at Parcevall Hall;
River Wharfe; Craven Arms

SIMON'S SEAT

At 1591ft/485m the summit of this popular landmark is a rocky boss that requires hands to attain, worth every effort for a dramatic bird's-eye view of the valley at Skyreholme. Subsidiary tops include Earl Seat and Lord's Seat. Best ascent route is through the Valley of Desolation from the Cavendish Pavilion.

Opposite: Earl Seat; Waterfall in the Valley of Desolation   Summit rocks; Simon's Seat from Appletreewick

BARDEN

Barden claims the Wharfe's finest bridge, and a tablet dates its restoration by Lady Anne Clifford 'at the charge of the whole West Riding' as 1676. Just above are the ruins of Barden Tower, built a hunting lodge with adjacent chapel by the powerful Cliffords of Skipton Castle. The redoubtable Lady Anne restored the tower in 1659 and spent much of her final years here until her death in 1676, the last of the Cliffords. Barden Moor is a vast playground both for the rambler and the less unobtrusive 'sportsman'. Above the intake walls encircling it, bracken flanks give way to heather and rough grass, where one can follow paths and tracks or roam free: Wordsworth's historic White Doe track to Rylstone is the only bridleway on the moor, an adventurous biking route.

Barden Bridge - complete with Robin; Chapel   Opposite: On the White Doe track; Barden Tower

THE STRID

At Strid Wood man and nature appear to happily co-exist as the Wharfe rushes spiritedly through glorious woodland. A splendid path network laid out in the 19th century has been maintained ever since by the Duke of Devonshire's estate. The Strid is the focal point as the river is forced through a narrow gritstone channel: lives have been lost in attempts to leap the foaming waters. The Cavendish Pavilion offers riverbank refreshments at the entrance.

The Strid   Opposite: Dawn over Strid Wood; Nuthatch; Strid Wood seasons

BOLTON ABBEY

Bolton Abbey is the name for the tiny village whose majestic riverside ruin is more correctly the Priory. This dates from 1154 and was built by Augustinian canons who moved here from Embsay. At the Dissolution the nave was spared, and survives to this day as the priory church of St Mary & St Cuthbert. Further interest includes adjacent Bolton Hall from the 17th century. On the main road are a Post office, shop, tearooms, bookshop and a grand example of a tithe barn. A fountain commemorates Lord Frederick Cavendish, assassinated in Phoenix Park, Dublin in 1882. Cavendish is the family name of the Dukes of Devonshire, proud owners of the estate but probably better known for their sumptuous seat at Chatsworth, in Derbyshire.

The Wharfe at Bolton Abbey

Architecture at Bolton Abbey:
Church; Hall; Priory

BOLTON BRIDGE

Shapely Bolton Bridge marks the Wharfe's departure from the National Park, and completion of the 1994 by-pass at last left this splendid old crossing in peace. The extension of a steam railway from Embsay has seen Bolton Abbey's restored station again echo to the sound, smell and sight of the trains of yesteryear. The Devonshire Arms Hotel bears the arms of the patriarchal family whose vast estate quietly and efficiently runs almost everything you see hereabouts. A delightfully sited cricket pitch sits between hotel and river.

Devonshire Arms; Dawn above Bolton Bridge
Opposite: Bolton Bridge; River Wharfe

Beamsley

This small settlement is best known for the moorland peak of Beamsley Beacon, at just 1296ft/395m a perfect mini-mountain with a fine bird's-eye view over the Bolton Bridge scene. Beamsley Hospital is an arrangement of almshouses founded in 1593 by the mother of Lady Anne Clifford. Archways flanked by six dwellings reveals the roundhouse, where from a central chapel seven rooms radiate, in their original use until recent times.

Beamsley Hospital, Beamsley Beacon

DRAUGHTON

An unassuming village featuring some lovely stone cottages, just above which on the edge of heathery Draughton Moor runs an ancient coaching road linking Ilkley and Skipton: an 18th century milestone survives. At Chelker Reservoir the removal of one of Britain's earliest windfarms has seen plans for taller replacements firmly rejected, a landmark decision for this quality landscape. Steam trains on the Embsay & Bolton Abbey Railway chug enthusiastically through the hollow of Draughton Bottom.

Slower days of travel:
Old milestone; Steam train;
Chelker Reservoir and Beamsley
Beacon from the coach road

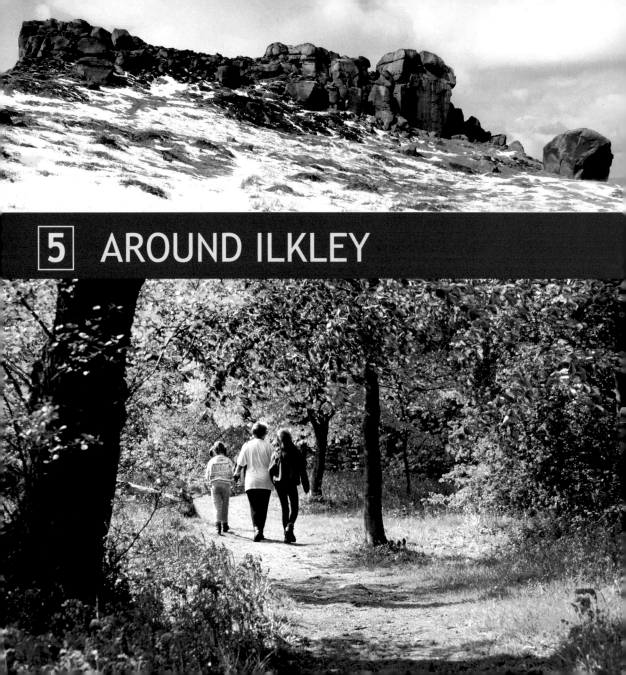

UNDER THE FAMOUS MOOR........

The Yorkshire anthem "On Ilkla Moor Baht'at" warns of the perils of roaming this iconic upland without adequate headgear, but woolly hat or not, this is very much a wonderful place to be. In truth Ilkley Moor is but one part of the massive Rombalds Moor, a lofty boundary between Wharfe and Aire. Its best known feature may be the Cow & Calf Rocks, but also worth seeking are its innumerable Bronze Age cup and ring marked boulders, its stone circles and the enigmatic Swastika Stone. The floral town of Ilkley sits in the shadow of its moor, blending shopping streets with historic features that include a Roman fort. Nearby Burley and Addingham also sit between moor and river, while Denton and Askwith occupy affluent parkland landscapes, where woodland and farmland give way to swathes of moorland that form a less frequented barrier between Wharfe and Washburn.   Burley; Middleton; Burley Moor   Opposite: Cow & Calf Rocks; Middleton Woods

ADDINGHAM

Addingham was the scene, in 1826, of a thousand-strong Luddite riot, an abortive attempt to break into the mill to smash powerlooms in this highest major mill settlement on the Wharfe. Its main street retains much bustle, while in a verdant corner where Town Beck gurgles under arched churchgoers' bridges, parts of St Peter's church date from medieval times. Just north of the village, the 1728 mansion of Farfield Hall contrasts with a modest Friends' Meeting House of 1689.

Opposite: Quaker meeting house; Fleece; Church   Rambling by the Wharfe; Farfield Hall

MIDDLETON

The extended environs of this farming hamlet high above the valley opposite Ilkley offer much of interest. Imposing Myddelton Lodge was the late 16th century home of the staunchly Roman Catholic Middletons until passing to the church a century ago: it is now back in private hands. Immersed in nearby woodland is Calvary, where carved stones representing the Stations of the Cross line a path to a grotto, a beautiful, peaceful location. A nearby milestone points to the moorland route to 'Rippon', while close by the river, Middleton Woods has many footpaths from which to appraise a spectacular springtime carpet of bluebells. Rising contrastingly high above are Middleton Moor and Langbar Moor.

Calvary scene at Myddelton
Lodge; Milestone
Opposite: Middleton Woods;
Trekking on Middleton Moor;
The Grey Stone, Langbar Moor

ILKLEY

The highest town on the Wharfe is a perfect stepping-stone between industrial conurbations and the joys of the Yorkshire Dales. This thriving town blends a workaday existence with that of a tourist venue, its spacious streets decorated by a tapestry of floral colour. All Saints' church has a 500-year old tower, but is best known for its Anglo-Saxon crosses, also a well-preserved effigy of 14th century knight Adam de Middleton. The church covers part of the site of the Roman fort of VERBEIA, built around 79 AD: evidence is restricted to a small section of preserved wall. Also by the church, the 16th century Manor House is a museum of local interest. Originally serving the packhorse trade, the Old Bridge was rebuilt after the 1673 flood that swept away many of the Wharfe's bridges. This and a ferry were replaced by the present bridge in 1904. The popular green spaces in between the two bridges are the townsfolk's memorial to their war dead.

Perched high on moorland overlooking the town, White Wells is a monument to Ilkley's early spa days. In the mid-19th century large hydros were built for people to take of the therapeutic waters, but a century earlier Squire Middleton built White Wells as a bath-house to enable townsfolk to enjoy a dip in the pure moorland spring water. Inside is a deep circular pool hollowed from the rock and fed by a cold mineral spring. Ilkley flourished as the 'Malvern of the North', and the Victorians revelled in the healing powers of its waters.

White Wells; Manor House; The Old Bridge

ILKLEY MOOR

This bracing tract of heather upland stands for all that is best about Yorkshire. Though only a part of all-embracing Rombalds Moor, Ilkley Moor draws folk from far beyond the Broad Acres. While gritstone occurs dramatically all over the moor, historically more significant are the stone circles, burial cairns, and the cup & ring markings that decorate many a dark boulder, abundant relics of the Bronze Age. On the escarpment from Woodhouse Crag to Windgate Nick is the enigmatic Swastika Stone, which shares the characteristics of symbols found in Scandinavia. Near the moor summit, Cowper's Cross (a former market cross) stands amid characterful boulders such as the Buck Stones and Thimble Stones.

Wharfedale from cup & ring marked rocks on Piper's Crag; Cowper's Cross

Heber's Ghyll; On Woodhouse Crag;
Swastika Stone; Buck Stones

Cow & Calf Rocks

These esteemed outcrops constitute one of Yorkshire's premier landmarks, and their roadside location sees them swarming with visitors. Also hugely popular with climbers, the main buttress of the Cow is so bold and uncompromising that most rock gymnasts will be found in the great bowl of the quarry round the back. Below the Cow is its offspring the Calf, whose scooped steps offer an easy angled scramble. Close by is a prominent hanging rock known as the Pancake Stone, its flat top awash with Bronze Age cup marks.

Below: The Pancake Stone

BURLEY-IN-WHARFEDALE

A popular village between Ilkley and Otley, Burley has a busy main street, a tall-spired church and a spacious green. Burley Woodhead is an exclusive scattering of houses high on the edge of Burley Moor. Portrayed at the Hermit Inn is 19th century character Job Senior, who at the age of 60 wed, with questionable motives, a much younger woman: on her demise her family threw down their cottage, so Job built a hut on the spot and lived in squalor as an object of curiosity. The moorland Twelve Apostles is a Bronze Age relic whose dozen stones form a neat circle on a well-chosen setting overlooking both Wharfedale and Airedale. Just beyond is the boundary stoop of Lanshaw Lad, inscribed with the year 1833 and still delineating the division between Ilkley Moor and Burley Moor.

Twelve Apostles; St Mary's church
Opposite: Lanshaw Lad; Hermit Inn;
Sheep gathering on Burley Moor

DENTON

This tiny village is based around a delightful little green backed by a row of stone cottages and old school. Denton Hall is an imposing mansion set within archetypal rolling parkland. The original house was for around 200 years home to the Fairfax family, of whom Sir Thomas Fairfax led the Parliamentarian forces at Marston Moor in 1644. The present hall dates from the 1770s, the work of John Carr. Atop the heathery sweep of Denton Moor is Lippersley Pike, whose large, hollow cairn is denoted as an antiquity.

Denton Hall   Lippersley Pike

ASKWITH

With near-neighbour Weston, these sleepy hamlets on the exclusive north bank of the Wharfe send farming slopes rising to their respective moors. Askwith has school and pub, while Weston hosts lovely All Saints church, once a private chapel to Weston Hall. Dating back to the 17th century, the hall was extended by the celebrated John Carr of York. Turner was a regular visitor here, as the long-time owners the Fawkes family were enthusiastic patrons of the great artist.

The Manor House, Askwith · Autumn at Weston

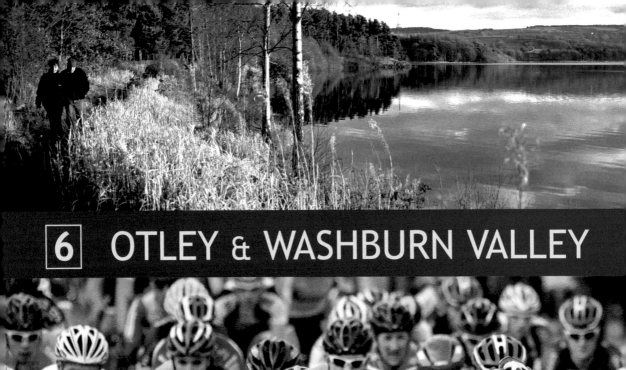

6 OTLEY & WASHBURN VALLEY

YORKSHIRE'S LAKE DISTRICT........

The Washburn Valley snakes down from high heather moorland to join the River Wharfe just downstream of Otley. Enviably sited beneath its lofty Chevin ridge and the Washburn moors, this exuberant market town has a refreshingly independent air and hosts a succession of colourful events throughout the year. The unsung Washburn is a victim of its setting, for its deep sides and handy location have seen it plundered for water catchment, its three Victorian reservoirs joined by capacious Thruscross in the 1960s. Tiny hamlets and scattered farms survive among the rolling pastures and woodland, and this remains a beautiful and popular objective for West Yorkshire ramblers.

Farm at Norwood; Old guidestone at Otley; Lake in old gravel pits below Otley
Opposite: Swinsty Reservoir; Otley cycle races

BLUBBERHOUSES

Blubberhouses boasts a jolly name and a reputation for the first snow-blocked road of winter, overseen by a landmark gritstone outcrop at Raven's Peak. The vast Blubberhouses Moor is crossed by a still evident Roman road, while a much more 'recent' milestone identifies an important trading route between Ilkley and Ripon. Overlooked by the elevated Stone House Inn, the mighty concrete dam at Thruscross holds back the youngest of the Washburn lakes, constructed as recently as 1966. Just to the east sits the eerie radome cluster at the military spying base of Menwith Hill.

Blubberhouses Moor and Thruscross Reservoir

Raven's Peak;
Milestone on
Blubberhouses
Moor; Looking
to Menwith Hill

FEWSTON

It is difficult now to imagine Fewston as the active community it was before the arrival in the 1870s of the twin-like Fewston and Swinsty reservoirs: both however offer attractive walking circuits above their tree-lined shores. St Lawrence's church boasts a solid 14th century tower, the rest rebuilt in 1697 after a fire, making it a rare example of church architecture of that period. It also houses the Washburn Heritage Centre.

Fewston Reservoir, church window and lambing time

Opposite: Swinsty Reservoir; Church

TIMBLE

This peaceful village sits on a broad ridge descending from the moors to the Washburn Valley, and the Timble Inn has long been a ramblers' favourite. Across the street is the former Robinson Gill Library and Free School, the gift in 1891 of a local lad who found fortune in America. Nearby Timble Gill Beck was the 17th century haunt of the Timble Witches, less infamous than their Pendle sisters but enough of a threat to paranoid locals to have faced trial at York. South of the village beyond the colourful moorland of Snowden Carr stand the remains of Dob Park Lodge, a 17th century hunting lodge from the old Forest of Knaresborough.

Dob Park Lodge; The Timble Inn in a different era (1993)

Timble, with pub and old library

The Washburn Valley from Snowden Carr

LEATHLEY

The scattered community of Leathley is centred on St Oswald's church, sat proudly on a knoll embowered in Scots Pine. It boasts a Norman tower and a richly decorated Norman door. Also on this brow are almshouses and the old school of 1769. Upstream is Lindley Wood Reservoir, above which the packhorse bridge of Dobpark Bridge, unofficial emblem of Washburn country, gracefully arches the River Washburn.

The farming community of Stainburn sits high above Leathley: its isolated, redundant church of St Mary dates back to Norman times.

Leathley stocks and almshouses;
Lindley Wood Reservoir
Opposite: Stainburn church; Dobpark Bridge

OTLEY

This buzzing little market town sits on the south bank of the Wharfe, and throws a long, sturdy bridge across the wide-flowing river. In this birthplace of celebrated cabinet-maker Thomas Chippendale, mid-May sees the colourful Otley Show herald the start of the county's 'show' season. A summer evening in early July sees the streets closed for a prestigious series of cycle races, and they're closed again in December for a popular Victorian market.

At All Saints church a memorial based on the portal of the nearby Bramhope rail tunnel honours the lives lost in its construction. The Jacobean old grammar school is centrally placed, while Otley remains proud of its stock of public houses. The small square still hosts weekly markets, while the livestock auction mart serves the district's farmers.

Memorial; Church; Victorian fair

Opposite: Bridge; Chippendale; Prize-winning cattle and the Airedale Beagles at Otley Show

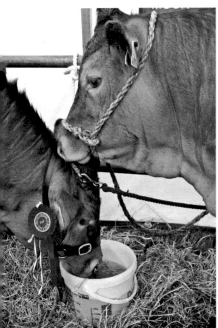

OTLEY CHEVIN

The bold ridge of Otley Chevin is a landmark boundary between Wharfe and Aire, but its dramatic northerly plunge ensures it is indelibly linked with the former, and in particular that town in its dark winter shadow. Its airy crest atop the colourful slopes of Beacon Hill Moor is gained by a ten-second hop from Surprise View car park, or more rewardingly in a gut-busting climb from the town centre. Either way, the reward is a

bird's-eye view of Otley as foreground to a far-reaching panorama from Great Whernside high in the Dales to Ferrybridge Power Station on the Aire flatlands. This has been the setting for many a bonfire, either to warn of approaching danger, or more usually to celebrate major events. It is also the location of a 30ft wooden cross erected annually to mark the start of Holy Week leading up to Easter.

Chevin Inn; 2013 Queen's Jubilee celebrations   Opposite: Chevin sunset; Easter cross; Otley from the Chevin

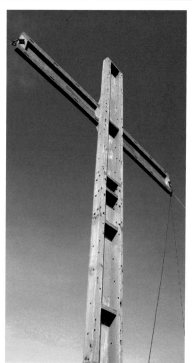

105

7 HAREWOOD to WETHERBY

AN OPULENT FAREWELL TO THE HILLS........

Spirit of Ecstasy at Harewood; Harewood hill climb; Wetherby Races

Opposite: Autumn at Harewood Park; Man and gritstone in harmony at Almscliff Crag

From one of Yorkshire's greatest stately houses to one of its many racecourse towns, this section known as the Wharfe Valley marks the river's departure from its cushion of rolling slopes. At Wetherby the Great North Road emphatically heralds the end of the Wharfe's diminishing contours, while Harewood boasts much more than its mansion, with an ancient castle, bird garden, deer park and colourful events. The timeless gritstone landmark of Almscliff Crag looks out over a string of charming villages, also watched over by an abundance of equally iconic Red kites quartering the skies.

POOL-IN-WHARFEDALE

This pleasant village is split by the incessant traffic rumbling along its groaning street. Pool Bank climbs above the village, and a former tollbar survives at the top of the old road. Its bridge is a major crossing point on the Wharfe for those bound for Harrogate and leafy North Yorkshire. The flat pastures immediately across it are the setting for Arthington Show, which rather quirkily is not only not held in its own village, but not even its own county! It is, however, a delightful country show on a scale to provide much of interest yet maintaining a distinctly 'local' feel.

Stocks and pub; Anglers' lake on an old gravel pit upstream

108

Animals are the stars at Arthington Show

ALMSCLIFF CRAG

This major Wharfe Valley landmark is prominent in views from all around the district. Sat among neatly packaged fields, it is a hugely popular venue for climbers, its rough gritstone offering scores of routes at all levels. Easily ascended from the rear is the crest of the major outcrop, High Man: its extensive panorama embraces the full girth of Rombalds Moor as well as the lesser-known moors north of Ilkley. Immediately below are further outcrops known as Low Man. Almost in its shadow is sleepy North Rigton, with the modest church of St John and village stocks on a little green opposite its pub.

KIRKBY OVERBLOW

    This hugely interesting village is clustered on an exposed ridge dividing the Wharfe and the Nidd, and overlooks a hollowed bowl falling to the former. Its name is likely derived from 'ore-blower', as iron smelting took place here in the 13th century. Two pubs survive, and All Saints church retains a 15th century tower. Close by, the roadside St Helen's Well is fed by a supply of spring water rising behind it: at one time the village was supplied by around 40 wells. There is a strong likelihood of a display of Red kites wheeling overhead.

Church; Red kite; Pub sign

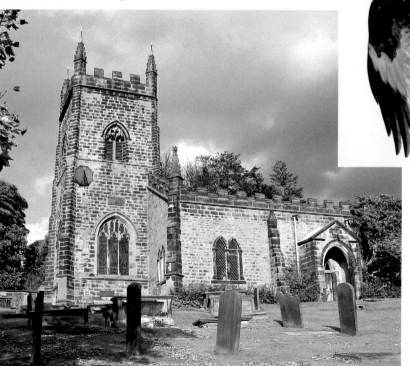

ARTHINGTON

This linear village straggles for a full mile along the valley beneath the steep, partly-wooded slopes of Arthington Bank. Its pub the Wharfedale is named from the long viaduct that spans the Wharfe: when the Otley branch existed, Arthington was a triangle of routes. A locally dominant landmark is the tall spire of St Peter's church, like Weeton's church directly across the river, the work of renowned Victorian architect Sir Giles Gilbert Scott. A mile further along the road is The Nunnery, a beautiful 16th century gritstone house on the site of a 12th century nunnery. Arthington's annual agricultural show takes place in neighbouring Pool, and is featured on page 109.

St Peter's church; The Nunnery; Farm mosaic

WEETON

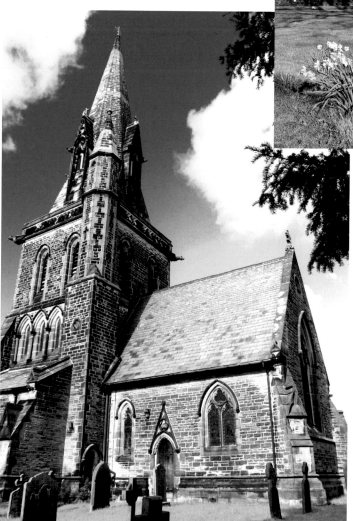

Sleepy Weeton is tucked away between the busy Bradford-Harrogate and Leeds-Harrogate roads. The Old Hall sits back from a spacious green, while the isolated church of St Barnabus boasts a spire that dominates the local landscape. Hidden in trees beside the riverbank at Rougemont Carr is an ancient bank with distinctive ditches: perhaps dating back at least to Anglo-Saxon times, this was also the site of a castle or fortified house of the Lords de L'Isle some 700 years ago.

Church; Green; Sloes in the hedgerows

HAREWOOD HOUSE

One of Yorkshire's premier stately homes, the seat of the Earl of Harewood dates from 1759, built on profits of the Lascelles family's West Indian sugar plantations. This magnificent house boasts a fine pedigree: designed by John Carr of York, interiors by Robert Adam, furniture by Thomas Chippendale, and grounds courtesy of Capability Brown. The resplendent rooms are particularly notable for housing an extensive art collection. Within the grounds is a bird garden, while numerous special interest events are organised. A splendid circular walk makes a circuit of Harewood Park, and the herds of deer that roam the grounds are almost certain to be encountered. The hugely successful release of previously endangered Red kites ensures almost guaranteed sightings of these magnificent birds of prey soaring above.

Never a dull moment at Harewood: Rolls-Royce, Harley-Davidson and traction engine rallies; Humboldt Penguin and Flamingo

HAREWOOD

Immediately outside the entrance to Harewood House, this estate village perches high above the Wharfe's final hilly miles before nearing the plains at Wetherby. Several weekends throughout the year see these slopes host colourful hill climbs, when all manner of sporty vehicles spiral their way up from the Wharfe meadows. The Harewood Arms stands amongst neat dwellings, while the redundant All Saints' church sits within the estate grounds, boasting medieval monuments and a bluebell-carpeted churchyard. A short concessionary path runs through the trees to the hidden but impressive remains of Harewood Castle, which dates from the mid 14th century. Harewood Bridge is a major crossing point of the Wharfe.

Opposite: Hill climb and Castle

Looking down on the Wharfe Valley; Red deer in Harewood Park

BARDSEY & EAST RIGTON

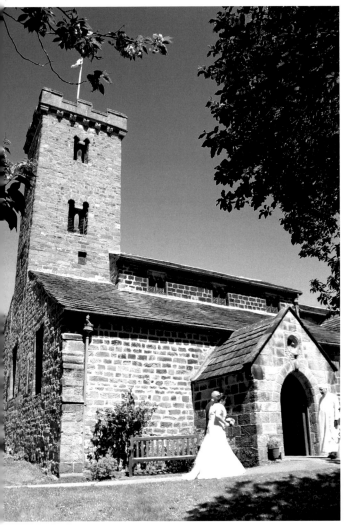

Leafy Bardsey is based around the church of All Hallows with its Anglo-Saxon tower, and other parts dating from Norman times. Despite being rebuilt down the centuries, the oldest part of the Bingley Arms is said to have survived for a thousand years, thus laying claim to being England's oldest pub. Bardsey is joined at the hip with East Rigton, a scattered settlement whose focal point is an attractive little green.

Spring wedding at Bardsey
and cyclists at East Rigton

East Keswick

East Keswick is the northern-most of a cluster of neighbouring villages that are distant rural satellites of the Leeds district. Central features include a West Riding roadsign and a working 'Leeds' clock on an adjacent building. Just north of the village are the last appreciable slopes that fall to the Wharfe.

Village cricket and springtime slopes above the Wharfe

LINTON

This well-to-do village just outside Wetherby has a triangular green sporting a canopied village pump, while the popular Windmill pub has a history as colourful as its floral embellishments. On the southern edge of the village, Linton Bridge forms a sturdy link with neighbouring Collingham.

Linton Bridge and village pump

COLLINGHAM

A busy village astride the staggered junction of two main roads, Collingham's lovely old church with surviving Saxon stonework still manages to glow in Magnesian limestone. Collingham Beck flows through to join the Wharfe in the attractive environs of Linton Bridge which separates - or links - these friendly neighbours.

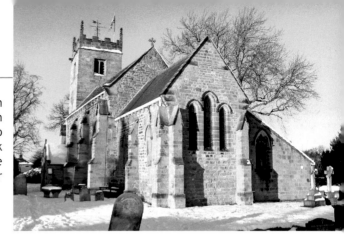

St Oswald's church and poppy-draped meadows

WETHERBY

This fine floral town on the north bank of the Wharfe was granted a market charter in 1240, and a market still takes place on Thursdays. Wetherby was at its busiest as a staging post on the Great North Road: precisely midway between London and Edinburgh, its main street would have been lined by coaching inns - some of which survive today. Happily a 1961 by-pass saw the A1 deflected east of town. The old bridge still carries most traffic into town, an elegant structure whose 13th century origins are still very evident when viewed from below. By the adjacent weir is a cogwheel rescued from an old mill.

Wetherby's focal point is the market place, in which stand the old town hall and the market hall containing the Shambles, built in 1811 by the Duke of Devonshire as butchers' shops. St James' church dates from 1841, while by the riverbank is a Georgian bath-house, where 200 years ago cold plunges were considered both fashionable and beneficial. The remains of an early 19th century lodge of the demolished Wetherby Grange stand by the entrance roundabout. The town has a century-old cinema, a silver band, and a cultural festival in late autumn. Wetherby is also home to one of Yorkshire's many celebrated racecourses.

Opposite: Church and Races

Lodge; Weir; Bridge and Shambles

8 TADCASTER to the OUSE

ESCAPE TO THE PLAINS........

The final miles of the Wharfe see it meander through arable fields where rape and poppies add colour to a subdued landscape interspersed with villages linked by narrow lanes. The more easterly sport characterful red pantiled roofs, while those further west are distinctive in the weathered grey of Magnesian limestone. The brewing town of Tadcaster has them in abundance, while neighbouring Boston Spa and Clifford have them in elegant style.

Cock Beck brings in a cluster of villages from the south, while redundant windmills overlook these sleepy backwaters in between Leeds and York supplying homes to city commuters. This region is certainly not without interest, from a Wars of the Roses battlefield to a wartime RAF airfield, from the Great North Road at Aberford and Bramham with their old coaching inns to silent subjugation to the Ouse at Wharfe's Mouth, a few miles south of York.

Pictorial inn signs at Tadcaster, Boston Spa and Appleton Roebuck; Turnpike milestones; Village pumps at Bolton Percy and Saxton

Opposite: Rapefield at Healaugh; Tadcaster Bridge

BRAMHAM

Bramham is an absorbing village amid rolling parkland, and was a major staging post in the days of the Great North Road. Various signs of more important times can be found, including former coaching inns, village cross, turnpike milestone, village pump and trough, and a grand old church. Bramham Park is a fine mansion dating from 1698 and set within delightful and extensive grounds. Its parkland hosts the contrasting but equally colourful annual events of the Leeds music festival and the internationally

recognised horse trials, an equestrian extravaganza. Bramham Moor was the site of a 1408 battle in which Henry IV's supporters put down a rebellion by the Percys.

Nature's tapestry; Village sign; Stables, Bramham Park

Bramham International Horse Trials: Pimms time, Dressage, Show jumping and summer hats

BOSTON SPA

This bustling street village in the heart of Magnesian limestone country has fine Georgian architecture lining its busy street. The name comes from the discovery of a mineral spring in 1744, and alongside the Wharfe, the Spa Baths survive as a group of lodge-type houses. Upstream, the cliffs of Jackdaw Crag rise from the water.

Boston Spa's quiet neighbours include Newton Kyme, whose Hall dates back to the 17th century: St Andrew's church within its parkland is part of a delightful timewarp where the BBC could make a period drama with little effort. Quietest is Wighill, which like Walton built its church upon a knoll. Thorp Arch is a village of spacious greens with its Victorian church stood aloof, while St Luke's church at characterful Clifford is joined by an imposing Catholic church.

The Wharfe at Jackdaw Crag;
Georgian housing; The Spa Baths

128

Four seasons
in the villages
around
Boston Spa:
St Peter's,
Walton;
All Saints,
Thorpe Arch;
Newton Kyme
Hall;
St Edward's,
Clifford

TADCASTER

The final town on the Wharfe is one of Britain's great brewing centres, the North's answer to Burton-on-Trent with three active breweries. 'Taddy' was the Roman CALCARIA, an indication of the importance of the local Magnesian limestone that also earned its brewing status. The Ark is a half-timbered merchant's house from the 15th century, while a grassy mound and ditch are all that remains of Tadcaster's 13th century castle. A defunct viaduct of 1849 spanning the river on two wide arches was the work of the 'Railway King' George Hudson of York, though financial difficulties meant it was little more than a folly.

The Ark; Individual sign outside Samuel Smith's brewery tap; St Mary's church and the Wharfe from the bridge
Opposite: Grandeur in stone at John Smith's brewery and the magnificent east window in St Mary's church

BARWICK-IN-ELMET

This sizeable village recalls the ancient kingdom of Elmet, and today is based around a tall maypole, the focus of triennial celebrations. Several pubs are in close attendance, along with historic All Saints church. Wendel Hill is the site of an Iron Age fort that over a millennium later was 'replaced' by a Norman motte and bailey of the de Lacys of Pontefract.

Wendel Hill and the maypole, and an inspired use of a redundant bus on the A64 at nearby Potterton

Aberford

Aberford is a classic street village a full mile in length, strung in peaceful solitude along what was once the bustling Great North Road. Aberford ceased to be a market town around 1800, and little remains of its coaching heyday. An old market cross stands on circular steps outside the parish church of St Ricarius, the only one in England so dedicated: recalling a 7th century French missionary, its spired tower is of Norman origin. Numerous attractive buildings stand back from a small, sloping green, while the remarkably ornate almshouses of 1844 were built by the Gascoigne family of nearby but since demolished Parlington Hall.

Church and almshouses

SAXTON

Focal point of this small village is the classic combination of church and pub, offering a scene that could only be English. The cramped interior of the tiny and ancient alehouse is an absolute delight. All Saints' church has a 15th century tower, and in the yard is the tomb of Lord Dacre, a Lancastrian slain at nearby Towton. A West Riding roadsign and the village pump survive.

LEAD

The redundant church of St Mary stands in the stark isolation of a field centre, though low grassy mounds identify the long abandoned village it once served. In the Battle of Towton this was a makeshift mortuary, while a predecessor of the Crooked Billet pub served as Yorkist headquarters during that infamous Roses slaughter. Nearby Lotherton Hall is in the hands of Leeds Council and open to the public, along with attractive grounds and a bird garden.

Lead Church and Lotherton Hall

Towton & Hazlewood

This otherwise unassuming village claims a big place in history due to the events of Palm Sunday 1461, when up to 30,000 mostly Lancastrian troops perished in a Wars of the Roses bloodbath amid foul weather. The deadliest battle on English soil saw Cock Beck run red with blood long after the fighting ended.

Across the beck from Towton is Hazlewood Castle, a majestic house of gleaming Magnesian limestone. For over eight centuries it was home of the influential Roman Catholic Vavasour family. Their 13th century manor house was fortified a century later, and today's largely 18th century building includes a chapel dating back to the late 13th century. The Vavasours left in 1908, and after late 20th century occupancy by Carmelite Friars, the Catholic connection ceased and the mansion was reborn as a hotel.

Towton battlefield

Hazlewood Castle

Healaugh

The dignified red-brick properties of this street village lead to a very distinctive knoll on which sits St John's church. A fine carved Norman doorway shares the accolades with wide panoramas. In its shadow is the 300-year old Old Hall.

Church and summer fields of oilseed rape

ULLESKELF

Ulleskelf sits close by the meandering bends of the Wharfe. A former windmill at Ulleskelf Mires on the outskirts dates from around 1770.

The adjacent, appropriately named hamlet of Kirkby Wharfe sits plum on the river's bank. Little more than the odd cottage and farm stand near the church of St John the Baptist, with the graves of 23 airmen from RAF Church Fenton. Alongside are the grounds of Grimston Park, a large estate set around a mansion of 1839, now multiple residences.

The Wharfe at Ulleskelf; Mill House, Ulleskelf

CHURCH FENTON

A village best known for RAF Church Fenton, an airfield opened in anticipation of World War Two conflict. Fighter planes were largely used in a defensive capacity to protect Northern cities. It remained a fighter base until 1959, after which it undertook pilot training, and was only vacated by the military in 2013. All Saints church is a fine Magnesian limestone cruciform building, while a tiny green features a medieval cross shaft.
Church in winter; Summer riot

BOLTON PERCY

This attractive little village on a flood-prone plain boasts a lovely corner featuring All Saints church and the unchanged Crown Inn. Sandwiched between is an outstanding, timber-framed 15th century gatehouse.   Gatehouse; Church; Wharfe

APPLETON ROEBUCK

A delightful village with a delightful name, Appleton Roebuck sits on the wide plain between Wharfe and Ouse. Focal point is a spacious green, while two pubs and two places of worship survive. Nearer the river, 300-year old Nun Appleton Hall stands on the site of a 12th century nunnery. Isolated in a field is the shell of an imposing 19th century windmill. Neighbouring Colton is the tiniest of street villages, yet retains a pub and a modest red-brick church.

Appleton windmill and ploughing patterns; Colton's pub

RYTHER

The Wharfe's last village is a peaceful spot with the Rythre Arms on its street and the historic All Saints church isolated among the fields. Less than two miles downstream is Wharfe's Mouth, where our river submits itself to the mighty Ouse. Normally a meek affair, flooding can see the confluence submerged beneath a vast lake where the parent river's overwhelmed flood embankment snakes eerily off into the sunset. My contrasting summer visit saw a cormorant float down the Wharfe atop a log which promptly got wedged on the bank precisely at the confluence.

Church; Flooded fields at Wharfe's Mouth
Opposite: Wharfe's Mouth in calmer times (Ouse in the foreground); Cormorant; There's a river under here...

INDEX

144